QUICK Source

Microsoft®
Windows XP
Professional

Getting Started

Logging On

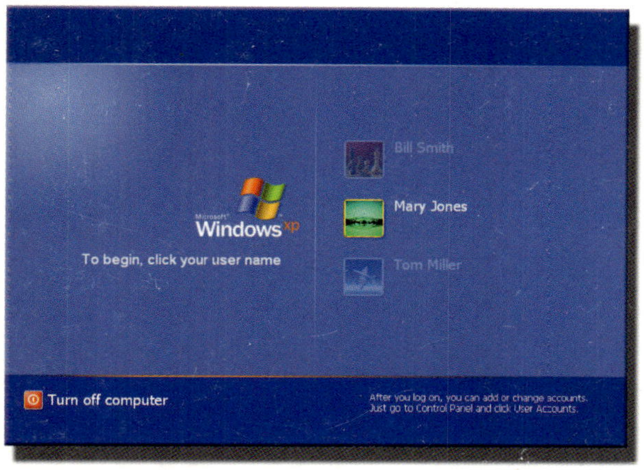

Depending on how your computer is set up, you will see the **Classic Logon** or the **Welcome Screen** (above) to log on to Windows XP.

Note: If your computer is connected to a network server, you may see your server logon screen instead.

Using the Taskbar

❶ **Quick Launch Bar** – provides single-click access to programs, files, and folders. (*Note: To hide or display the Quick Launch bar, right-click the taskbar and select **Properties** from the pop-up menu. On the **Taskbar** tab, check or clear the **Show Quick Launch** box. Click the **OK** button when you are done.*)

❷ **Taskbar buttons** – enable the user to switch quickly between open windows, programs, and documents.

❸ **Notification Area** – contains icons for active and urgent notifications, as well as the current time and sound controls.

NEW

Taskbar Grouping

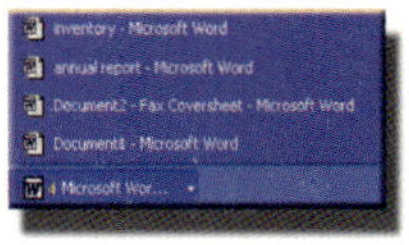

Since the Taskbar can become crowded with buttons, Windows has introduced Taskbar Grouping to its XP operating system. For example, if you are working on six documents and four of them are Word documents, the four Word document taskbar buttons are grouped into one button. Click the button to select which document you want to view.

Taskbar Notification Area

The Taskbar Notification area contains icons for events, such as when you receive new e-mail or an instant message, or when you need to run the virus checker. Since this area can become crowded, buttons will be hidden when not in use.

To view all buttons contained in the **Taskbar Notification** area, click the arrow button.

*Note: To customize the behavior of the notification icons, right-click the **Taskbar** and select **Properties** from the pop-up menu. Click the **Taskbar** tab to make changes to the Taskbar.*

Using the Desktop Cleanup Wizard

NEW

The Desktop Cleanup Wizard removes unused shortcut icons from your desktop. The Wizard runs automatically every 60 days.

To start or make changes to the Wizard:

1. Right-click an empty area of the Windows desktop.
2. Select **Properties** from the pop-up menu.
3. Click the **Desktop** tab.
4. Click the **Customize Desktop** button.
5. Check or clear the **Run Desktop Cleanup Wizard every 60 days** box, as desired.
6. To start the Wizard manually, click the **Clean Desktop Now** button. Follow the Wizard to clean up your desktop.
7. Click the **OK** button.
8. Click the **OK** button to close the **Display Properties** window.

Working with Windows

Each window has a **Title Bar** containing the name of the window or folder, a **Minimize** button, a **Maximize** button, a **Close** button, and, when the window is maximized, a **Restore Down** button.

- **Minimize** – hides the window from view. You can restore the window by clicking on its Taskbar button.
- **Maximize** – enlarges the window to full-screen view.
- **Close** – closes the window completely.
- **Restore Down** – restores a maximized window to its previous size.

Taking a Screen Picture

- *To take a picture of your desktop*, press the **Print Screen** key on your keyboard. To take a picture of only the active window, press **Alt + Print Screen**.
- *To paste the image into a document*, open the document and select **Paste** from the **Edit** menu.

Arranging Open Windows

1. Right-click an empty area on the **Taskbar**.
2. Select **Cascade Windows**, **Tile Windows Horizontally**, or **Tile Windows Vertically** from the pop-up menu.

*Note: To undo the arrangement and restore windows to their previous state, right-click an empty area of the **Taskbar** and select **Undo Cascade** or **Undo Tile** from the pop-up menu.*

Reducing Open Windows

To reduce all open windows to **Taskbar** buttons, click the **Show Desktop** button, located on the **Quick Launch** portion of the **Taskbar**. You can also reduce open windows by right-clicking the **Taskbar** and selecting **Show the Desktop** from the pop-up menu.

Start Menu

Using the Start Menu

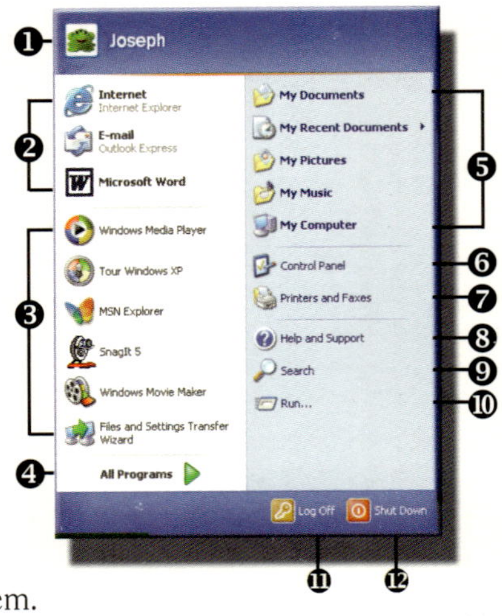

❶ **User Name** – displays the name of the current user.

❷ **Pinned Items List** – displays shortcuts to the programs that you have "pinned" to the Start menu.

❸ **Most Frequently Used Programs List** – displays shortcuts to the programs you use most frequently.

❹ **All Programs** – displays shortcuts to all programs loaded on your Windows system.

❺ **Folder Shortcuts** – opens the corresponding folder or location.

❻ **Control Panel** – opens the Control Panel, where you can make changes to display and system settings.

❼ **Printers and Faxes** – opens the Printers and Faxes window, where you can work with and install printers.

❽ **Help and Support** – opens the Help and Support Center, where you can access Help topics, tutorials, troubleshooting, and other support services.

❾ **Search** – opens the Search window, where you can search for files, folders, and applications.

❿ **Run** – opens the Run window, where you can open a program, folder, document, or Internet site.

⓫ **Log Off** – gives you the ability to log off of Windows and let another user log on.

⓬ **Shut Down** – gives you options for shutting down.

Note: To customize the ***Start*** *menu, right-click the* ***Start*** *button and select* ***Properties*** *from the pop-up menu.*

Pinning a Program

When you "pin" a program to the Start menu, the program's shortcut will remain on the Start menu.

1. Right-click the program icon as it appears in the **Start** menu, **Windows Explorer**, **My Computer**, or on the **Desktop**.
2. Select **Pin to Start Menu** from the pop-up menu.

Accounts

Setting Up a New Account

Set up and manage accounts for everyone who uses your computer.

1. Select **Control Panel** from the **Start** menu.
2. *In* ***Category*** *view*, click the **User Accounts** shortcut. *In* ***Classic*** *view*, double-click the **User Accounts** icon.
3. In the **User Accounts** window, click the **Create a new account** shortcut.
4. Enter a name for the account in the space provided. Click the **Next** button.
5. Select whether the user will have **Computer Administrator** access or **Limited** access. Details about each account type appear when you place the mouse pointer on the account type name.
6. Click the **Create Account** button.

Note: In the ***User Accounts*** *window, click the account name to make changes to an account.*

Changing Users without Logging Off

1. Select **Log Off** from the **Start** menu.
2. Click the **Switch User** button.
3. In the **Welcome** window, click the new user's icon.

Note: If you are not set up to use the Switch User feature, you will not see the ***Switch User*** *button in Step 2. Instead, click the* ***OK*** *button to log off.*

Windows Explorer

Use the Windows Explorer feature to "explore" your computer. You can view the contents of your computer, search for documents, save your favorite places, view your history, and view your folders in a hierarchical structure.

Opening Windows Explorer

Right-click the **My Computer** icon, located on your **Start** menu, and select **Explore** from the pop-up menu.

Using Windows Explorer

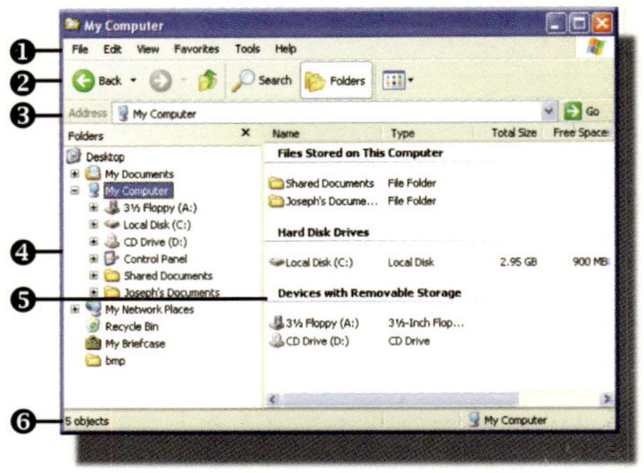

❶ **Menu Bar** – contains all tools for use with Windows Explorer.

❷ **Standard Toolbar** – contains tools for viewing and navigating.

❸ **Address Bar** – displays the location of the selected folder, drive, network, or Web site.

❹ **Explorer Bar** – displays your folders in hierarchical format. You can also select different Explorer bars for searching, saving favorite locations, accessing media, and viewing your history.

❺ **Contents Pane** – displays the contents of the item selected in the Explorer bar.

❻ **Status Bar** – displays size and status information about the selected item.

Note: To hide or display toolbars or bars, select the item from the ***View*** *menu.*

Selecting an Explorer Bar

You can choose from five different Explorer bars: **Search**, **Favorites**, **Media**, **History**, or **Folders**. To select a bar, select **Explorer Bar** from the **View** menu and select a bar from the resulting menu.

Using the Toolbar

Back – goes to the previously-viewed locations.

Forward – goes forward to locations after moving backwards.

Up – opens the folder one level up.

Search – opens the Search Companion.

Folders – opens the Folders Explorer bar.

Views – provides a list of ways to view items displayed in the Contents pane.

Control Panel

The Control Panel is the command center for your computer, controlling the way Windows looks and behaves. Customize your work environment by making changes to the Control Panel settings.

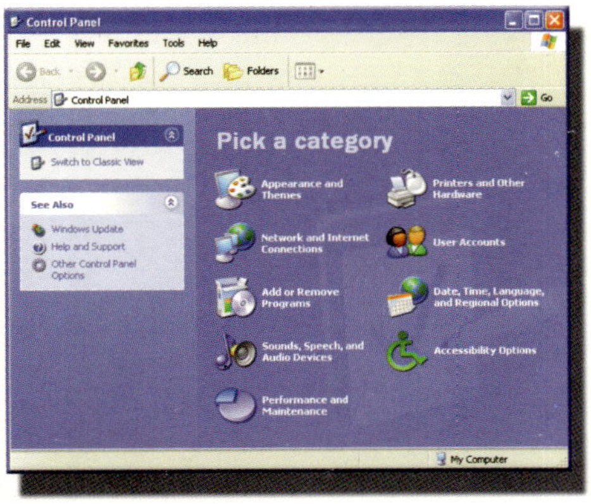

Using the Control Panel

To open the Control Panel, select **Control Panel** from the **Start** menu.

- *If you are using **Category** view*, you will see Control Panel items arranged by category. To view more information about a category, place the mouse pointer over the category name and a description will appear. To open an item, click once on the item's icon or name.
- *If you are using **Classic** view*, you will see icons for all items contained in the Control Panel. To view more information about an item, place the mouse pointer over the item and a description will appear. To open an item, double-click the item icon.

*Note: To switch between **Category** view and **Classic** view, click the **Switch To Category View** or **Switch to Classic View** shortcut in the **Tasks** pane.*

Setting Up the Task Manager

The Task Manager automatically performs scheduled tasks. You select the program you want Windows to run and then schedule it for a convenient time.

1. To open the Control Panel, select **Control Panel** from the **Start** menu.
2. *In **Category** view*, click the **Performance and Maintenance** shortcut. Then, click the **Scheduled Tasks** shortcut. *In **Classic** view*, double-click the **Scheduled Tasks** icon.
3. Double-click the **Add Scheduled Task** icon.
4. Click the **Next** button to start the **Scheduled Task Wizard**.
5. Select the program you want Windows to run.
6. Click the **Next** button.
7. Enter a name for the task in the space provided.
8. Select how often you want Windows to perform this task.
9. Click the **Next** button.
10. Select detailed time and date information, as applicable.
11. Click the **Next** button.
12. Enter a user name and password in the spaces provided.
13. Click the **Next** button.
14. Review the task information. Click the **Back** button to return to previous screens to make changes. Click the **Finish** button when done.

Adding a Printer

1. Select **Printers and Faxes** from the **Start** menu. (*If **Printers and Faxes** is not available on the **Start** menu, locate **Printers and Faxes** in the **Control Panel**.*)
2. Click the **Add a printer** shortcut in the **Printer Tasks** pane. The **Add Printer Wizard** will appear.
3. Follow the Wizard to set up your printer.
4. Click the **Finish** button when done.

Setting a Default Printer

1. Select **Printers and Faxes** from the **Start** menu.
2. Right-click the printer you want to make your default printer.
3. Select **Set as Default Printer** from the pop-up menu.

Getting Help

Using the Help and Support Center

- *To open the **Help and Support Center***, select **Help and Support** from the **Start** menu. The **Help and Support Center** home page will appear.
- *To browse by category or task*, click a category or task item in the **Help and Support Center** home page.

Using Index

1. To search using the **Index**, click the **Index** [Index] button, located on the **Navigation** bar.
2. Enter a keyword in the **Type in the keyword to find** box.
3. Select a matching item from the list box.
4. Click the **Display** button.

Note: You can also use the scroll bars on the list box to browse the index manually.

Using Search

1. To search using the **Search** box, enter a word or phrase in the **Search** box.
2. Click the **Start searching** button or press the **Enter** key.
3. Select a topic from the resulting list.

Using Contents

Click the **Locate in Contents** [Locate in Contents] button to locate a help page in the **Contents** list. When working in the **Contents** list, you can view help contents in a hierarchical format.

Remote Assistance

NEW

When you are having problems with your computer, you can use Remote Assistance to invite a friend or computer expert to access your computer and fix your problem. This person can view your screen as if sitting in front of your computer – even when miles away.

To request help using Remote Assistance:

1. Select **Help and Support** from the **Start** menu.
2. Click the **Invite a friend to connect to your computer with Remote Assistance** shortcut.
3. Follow the directions provided to set up Remote Assistance.

*Note: There are several requirements needed to be able to use Remote Assistance. For example, both users must use either Windows Messenger or a MAPI-compliant e-mail account (e.g. Outlook or Outlook Express), must both be connected to the Internet, and must be running compatible operating systems. See the **Help and Support Center** for more information.*

Files and Folders

Creating a New Folder

1. In **Windows Explorer**, go to the location where you want to create a new folder.
2. Select **New** from the **File** menu.
3. Select **Folder** from the resulting menu.
4. Enter a name for the folder in the space provided.
5. Press the **Enter** key.

Renaming a File or Folder

1. Right-click the file or folder you want to rename.
2. Select **Rename** from the pop-up menu.
3. Enter a new name for the file or folder in the space provided.
4. Press the **Enter** key.

Renaming a Series of Files

1. Select the files you want to rename.
   - *To select a series of files*, click once on the first file in the series, hold the **Shift** key and click the last file in the series.
   - *To select nonadjacent files*, hold the **Ctrl** key and click once on each file you want to select.
   - *To select all files*, press **Ctrl + A**.
2. Select **Rename** from the **File** menu.
3. Enter a new name in the space provided.
4. Press the **Enter** key. All files in the series will be named in sequence, using the name you typed. For example, if you type **Office Picnic Pictures**, the files will be named **Office Picnic Pictures (1)**, **Office Picnic Pictures (2)**, and so on.

Deleting a File or Folder

1. Right-click the file or folder you want to delete.
2. Select **Delete** from the pop-up menu.
3. Click the **Yes** button to confirm the deletion. The item will be sent to the **Recycle Bin**.

*Note: To permanently delete an item, click once on the item and then press **Shift + Delete**.*

Restoring Items in the Recycle Bin

1. Double-click the **Recycle Bin** icon, located on your desktop, to open the **Recycle Bin**.
2. Click once on the file or folder you want to restore.
3. Click the **Restore this item** shortcut in the **Recycle Bin Tasks** pane. Or, right-click the item and select **Restore** from the pop-up menu.

*Note: To permanently delete items in your **Recycle Bin**, click the **Empty the Recycle Bin** shortcut in the **Recycle Bin Tasks** pane.*

Changing the Program Used to Open a File

1. Right-click the file you want to open in a different program.
2. Select **Properties** from the pop-up menu.
3. On the **General** tab, click the **Change** button.
4. Click the name of the program you want to use to open this file.
5. Click the **OK** button.
6. Click the **OK** button to close the **Properties** window.

*Note: To quickly change the program used to open a file, right-click the file, select **Open With** from the pop-up menu, and select a program from the resulting menu.*

Applying Folder Settings to All Folders

1. In **Windows Explorer**, select a preferred view from the **View** menu (i.e. **Thumbnails**, **Tiles**, **Icons**, **List**, or **Details**).
2. Select **Folder Options** from the **Tools** menu.
3. On the **View** tab, click the **Apply to All Folders** button.
4. Click the **Yes** button to confirm the change.
5. Click the **OK** button to close the **Folder Options** window.

Using My Pictures & My Music

Windows provides folders designed to store and organize your pictures and music. These folders contain tools for working with your media items.

1. Select **My Music** or **My Pictures** from the **Start** menu.
2. Do one of the following:
   - *To open the item*, double-click the item.
   - *To select from a list of options*, right-click the item and select an action (e.g. **Preview**, **Edit**, or **Print** the picture or **Play** the music item.)
   - *To perform an action listed in the **Tasks** pane*, click the task. (e.g. **Play All**, **Print Pictures**, or **View as Slide Show**.)

Hiding a File or Folder

1. Right-click the file or folder you want to hide.
2. Select **Properties** from the pop-up menu.
3. On the **General** tab, check the **Hidden** box.
4. Click the **OK** button.

*Note: To view hidden files and folders, select **Folder Options** from the **Tools** menu in any folder window. On the **View** tab, click the **Show hidden files and folders** button (located in the **Hidden files and folders** section). Click the **OK** button when done.*

Sending a File or Folder

Use the Send To feature to send a file or folder to a disk or folder, to a mail recipient, or to the desktop as a shortcut.

1. Right-click the file or folder you want to send.
2. Select **Send To** from the pop-up menu.
3. Select a destination from the resulting menu.
4. Enter additional information, as needed.

Compressing Files and Folders

Windows XP makes it easy for you to compress your files and folders. Compressed folders are convenient when you want to send large files as e-mail attachments or save files to a disk. Also, they keep your files safe from contamination as they travel via e-mail or Internet.

1. Right-click the file or folder you want to compress.
2. Select **Send To** from the pop-up menu.
3. Select **Compressed (zipped) Folder** from the resulting menu. A "zipped" folder will appear, containing your compressed file or folder.

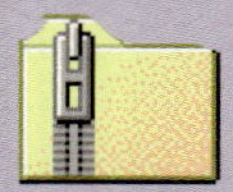

Working with a Compressed Folder

- *To open a compressed folder to view its contents*, double-click the folder.
- *To extract the contents of the folder*, right-click the folder and select **Extract All** from the pop-up menu. Follow the directions provided by the **Extraction Wizard**.

Search

Searching for a File or Folder

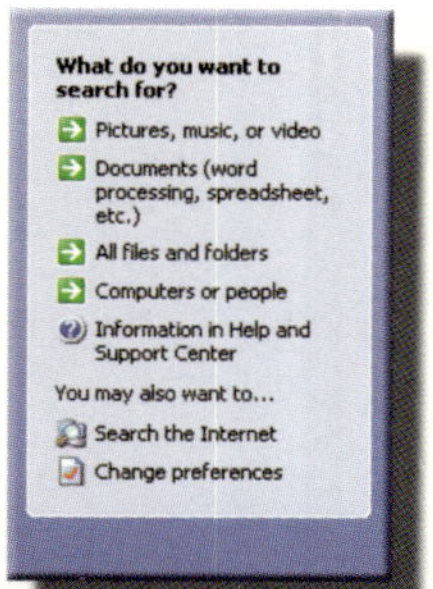

1. In **Windows Explorer**, click the **Search** button, or press **Ctrl + E**.
2. In the **Search Companion**, click the **All files and folders** shortcut.
3. Enter search information in the spaces provided.
4. Click the arrow on the **Look in** box and select the location you want to search.
5. To enter more search details, click the double down arrow buttons.
6. Click the **Search** button to start your search. A list of items matching the search criteria will appear in the **Contents** pane.
7. Double-click an item to open it. If your search was not successful, select another search option from the **Search Companion**.

Searching for Media Items

Windows can search for all pictures, music, and video stored on your computer.

1. In **Windows Explorer**, click the **Search** button, or press **Ctrl + E**.
2. In the **Search Companion**, click the **Pictures, music, or video** shortcut.
3. Check the boxes for the types of items you want to search for.
4. Enter any file name information in the text box, if desired. If you do not enter any file name information, Windows will find all media objects of the selected type(s).
5. Click the **Search** button. A list of media items will appear in the **Contents** pane.
6. Double-click an item to open it. If your search was not successful, select another search option from the **Search Companion**.

Searching the Internet

1. In **Windows Explorer**, click the **Search** button, or press **Ctrl + E**.
2. In the **Search Companion** pane, click the **Search the Internet** shortcut.
3. In the text box, enter a description of what you are looking for.
4. Press the **Enter** key.
5. If you are prompted to be more specific, enter additional information in the text box.
6. A search engine will appear, listing sites that should contain the information you are looking for. Click a site name to view that site.

History and Favorites

Using the History Bar

Use the History bar to quickly access recently-viewed files, folders, and sites.

1. In **Windows Explorer**, select **Explorer Bar** from the **View** menu and select **History** from the resulting menu, or press **Ctrl + H**.
2. Click the **View** button on the **History** bar.
3. Select a view from the resulting menu.
4. Click an item to open it.

Saving a Favorite Place

When you save your favorite file locations, sites, and searches when using Windows Explorer, you make them easier to find in the future.

1. When you have opened a location or run a search that you want to save in your Favorites list, select **Add to Favorites** from the **Favorites** menu.
2. Enter a name for your item in the **Name** box.
3. To select a **Favorites** folder to save your item in, click the **Create in** button and select a folder from the folder list.
4. Click the **OK** button when done.
5. To open a Favorites item, select the item from the **Favorites** menu.

Programs

Adding a Program to Your Computer

1. Select **Control Panel** from the **Start** menu.
2. *In **Category** view*, click the **Add or Remove Programs** shortcut.
   *In **Classic** view*, double-click the **Add or Remove Programs** icon.
3. Click the **Add New Programs** button.
4. Click the **CD or Floppy** button.
5. Follow the directions provided to install the new program.

Changing or Removing a Program

1. Select **Control Panel** from the **Start** menu.
2. *In **Category** view*, click the **Add or Remove Programs** shortcut.
   *In **Classic** view*, double-click the **Add or Remove Programs** icon.
3. Click the **Change or Remove Programs** button.
4. Select the program you want to change or remove.
5. *To change a program*, click the **Change/Remove** or the **Change** button.
   To remove a program, click the **Change/Remove** or the **Remove** button.
6. Follow the directions provided to change or remove the program.

Starting and Quitting a Program

- *To start a program*, select the program from the **Start** menu. If you do not see the program you want to start, select **All Programs** from the **Start** menu and select the program from the resulting menu.
- *To quit a program*, select **Exit** from the program's **File** menu, or click the **Close** button, located in the upper right corner of the program window's **Title Bar**.

Using Tasks

NEW

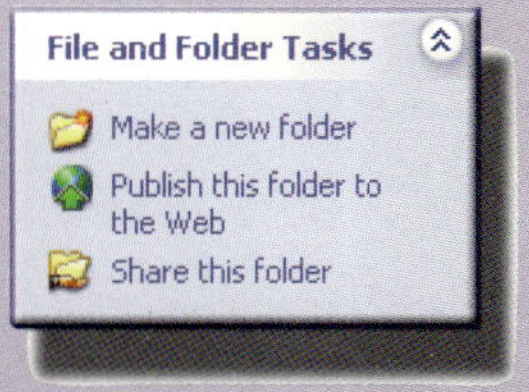

The Tasks pane contains shortcuts to common functions you use in the selected location. For example, when you are in the **My Pictures** folder, the **Tasks** pane gives you one-click access to viewing your pictures as a slide show. Also, in the **My Computer** folder, you can quickly view system information, add or remove programs, or change a setting. Click a task in the **Tasks** bar to perform the task.

*Note: In **Windows Explorer**, the **Explorer Bar** covers the **Tasks** pane. Click the **Close** button on the **Explorer Bar** to view the **Tasks** pane.*

Customizing

Using Themes

Themes unify and clean up your desktop. Use themes to apply a background and matching screen saver, icons, windows, mouse pointers, and sounds. Each user on your computer can have a different theme.

1. Right-click a blank area of the **Desktop**.
2. Select **Properties** from the pop-up menu.
3. On the **Themes** tab, select a theme from the **Theme** drop-down list. (*Note that you can select the **Windows Classic** style, which looks more like desktops in previous versions of Windows.*)
4. Click the **OK** button when done.

System Restore

Use System Restore to undo harmful changes to your computer. Restore returns your computer to a "restore point." You will not lose recent work, documents, e-mail, or history and favorite lists. System Restore is also reversible.

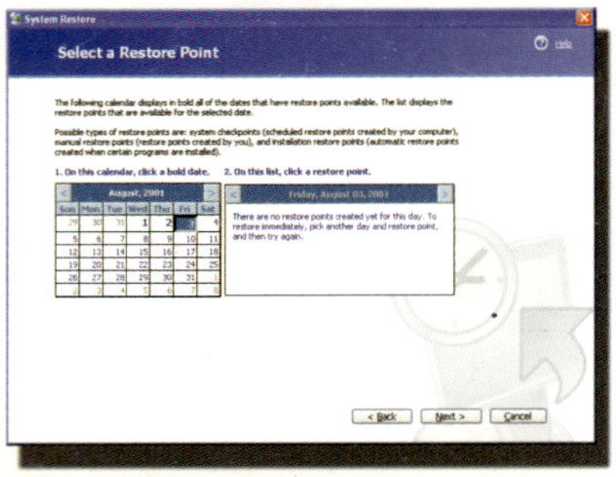

1. Select **All Programs** from the **Start** menu.
2. Select **Accessories** from the resulting menu.
3. Select **System Tools** from the resulting menu.
4. Select **System Restore** from the resulting menu. The **System Restore** window will appear.
5. Select whether you want to restore you computer to an earlier time or create a restore point.
6. Click the **Next** button.
7. Follow the directions provided by **System Restore**.

QUICK Source

To order call toll-free 1-888-280-0424.

Visit our Web site: **www.resourcenetwork.com**

Shortcuts

Common Windows XP Shortcut Keys

Activate **Menu** bar in programs	**F10**
Carry out menu operation	**Alt + letter underlined**
Copy	**Ctrl + C**
Cut	**Ctrl + X**
Delete	**Delete**
Display **Start** menu	**Ctrl + Esc**
Display the **Shortcut** menu	**Shift + F10**
Find	**Ctrl + F**
Help	**F1**
New	**Ctrl + N**
Open	**Ctrl + O**
Paste	**Ctrl + V**
Print	**Ctrl + P**
Quit/Exit	**Alt + F4**
Refresh	**F5**
Rename	**F2**
Save	**Ctrl + S**
Select All	**Ctrl + A**
Switch between open programs	**Alt + Tab**
Undo	**Ctrl + Z**
View Item Properties	**Alt + Enter**

Windows Explorer Shortcut Keys

Display the bottom of the active window.	**End**
Display the top of the active window.	**Home**
Display all subfolders under the selected folder.	**Asterisk on numeric keypad (*)**
Display the contents of the selected folder.	**Plus Sign on numeric keypad (+)**
Collapse the selected folder.	**Minus Sign on numeric keypad (-)**
Collapse current selection if it's expanded, or select parent folder.	**Left Arrow (←)**
Display current selection if it's collapsed, or select first subfolder.	**Right Arrow (→)**
Refresh	**F5**
Alternate focus between left and right panes and the Address Bar	**F6**
Copy a file	**Ctrl while dragging a file**
Create a shortcut	**Ctrl + Shift while dragging a file**
Delete an item immediately without placing it in the Recycle Bin	**Shift + Delete**

Using the Windows Logo Key

You can use the following keyboard shortcuts with any keyboard that includes the Windows Logo key.

Cycle through the buttons on the Taskbar	**WINDOWS + Tab**
Display Find: All Files	**WINDOWS + F**
Display Find: Computer	**Ctrl + WINDOWS + F**
Display Help	**WINDOWS + F1**
Display the Run command	
Displ	
Displ	
Displ	
Minin	

9781930674981